J. P. Tarcher, Inc., Los Angeles
Distributed by St. Martin's, New York

Calories Don't Count When...

Sara Parriott

Copyright © 1979 by Sara Parriott
All rights reserved.
Library of Congress Catalog Card No.: 79-84900
Distributor's ISBN: 0-312-90453-3
Publisher's ISBN: 0-87477-105-6

Design by Educational Graphics
Manufactured in the United States of America
Published by J. P. Tarcher, Inc.
9110 Sunset Blvd., Los Angeles, Calif. 90069

Published simultaneously in Canada by Thomas Nelson & Sons Limited,
81 Curlew Drive, Don Mills, Ontario M3A 2R1

10 9 8 7 6 5 4 3 2 1
First Edition

Introduction

Like countless people, I have spent a good part of each day torturing myself about my weight and wishfully thinking it would just go away. I have spent days wondering how many chins I would have when I got older and nights lying in bed gazing at my stomach, wishing that just once I could see past it to my hipbones. Three hundred and sixty-five days a year I made a solemn vow to start my diet the very next day.

This took much of the joy out of eating. Eventually I was incapable of letting one mouthful slip by without mentally totaling up its caloric content. I was a living, breathing Calorie Calculator. And I lived and breathed in constant torment.

You would think that my meticulous observation of caloric intake would make me a slender, healthy person, not to mention one who was strong willed and goal oriented. But after twenty-three years it had not. Then, a few weeks after my twenty-third birthday, on the very day that I reached the 20,378,412 calorie mark, I stood gazing at pictures of a party, trying to convince myself that everyone looks ten pounds heavier in photographs. I finally accepted the fact that counting calories was getting me nowhere. Dieting as I knew it was not working. Something had to be done. Someone had to be the pioneer.

I knew I could no longer depend upon external authorities. But what about me? I was probably as much of an authority as anybody. Who else knew that a parboiled kumquat contained 27 calories? Or that a prolonged session of nail cutting used up 11?

I started by reviewing all the previous diet plans I had been on—Stillman, Atkins, Scarsdale, Mayo Clinic, Weight Watchers, "sensible," and so on. I looked for a common denominator (besides the fact that they were all restrictive and depressing). What was it about these diets that had made them fail for me—and for millions of others? I burned thousands of calories looking for the answer, and, finally, perseverance paid off. I found it.

In all these diets the dieter became an obsessive observer of *physical scientific factors*. Each diet had its carefully thought out, scientifically tested scheme—metabolic rates, chemical interactions, flushing wastes, breakdown of fat cells, retention percentages, carbohydrate graphs, protein lists—all of it just wishful thinking decked out in scientific robes. Clearly these weights and measures weren't enough. They all left out one thing. *The Unknown*.

That was it! The Mysterious! The Uncertain! ESP! Astral Planes! Auras! Mandalas! How could everyone have missed it? Breakthrough science acknowledges it, religions are based on it, relationships couldn't survive without it. Millions make their living exploiting it. Why was it not part of dieting?

In search of The Unknown, I delved into the occult sciences and realms of consciousness. Maybe some sort of mantra before each meal. Or a pyramid on top of the refrigerator. I studied every book for The Answer. I spoke to all those in The Know. I searched in the spaceless, placeless, timeless dimensions—no easy task. Finally, exhausted, I turned in the Right Direction, to the acknowledged basis for *controlling* The Unknown—Positive Thinking.

The question was, how could I turn all that Wishful Thinking (that which takes up a large portion of every weight watcher's time) into Positive Thinking? How could I harness that positive energy into melting pounds away?

The answer was as clear as the question. Write a book! Nothing is more believable than a book (even one with a soft cover), and *believing* is the foundation of Positive Thinking. Give people something to hold on to, to put under their pillows or to carry around with them, a physical object that would help them focus their consciousness and obliterate calories!

So that's what I have done. I've written down and illustrated all those concepts you have subconsciously known but have not integrated into your being as the truth. I've collected all those situations when you *knew* calories didn't count but, because you did not apply visualization and Positive Thinking, your body didn't get the full benefit of your knowledge. Now that's a thing of the past.

The truth shall make you calorie free.

Sara Parriott

you don't eat the bun,

. . . it would have gone to waste

. . . you try something new

. . . and it tasted terrible

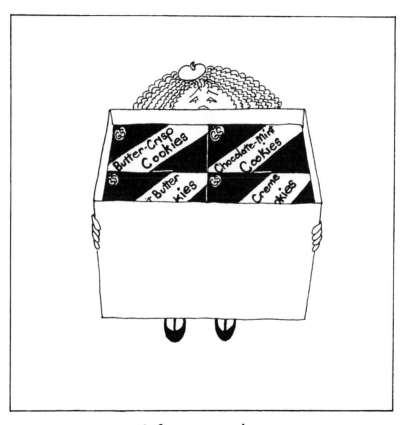

. . . it's for a good cause

. . . no one sees you

you're waiting

YOU'RE
IN EXTREME
TEMPERATURES

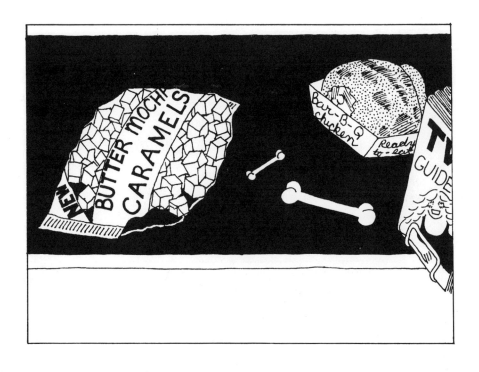

**YOU ONLY
EAT HALF**

R_X

It's for
medicinal
reasons

. . . you've worked for it

. . . you only have coffee

. . . it's salad

YOU'VE JUST EXERCISED

. . . you don't pay for it

. . . or you eat off someone else's plate

it's HEALTH Food

you share it.

. . . you can't see what you're eating

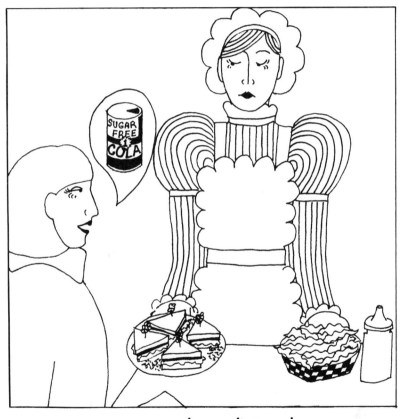

. . . you order a diet soda

it's BURNT

YOU ONLY EAT THE BROKEN ONES

. . . it makes the bill come out even

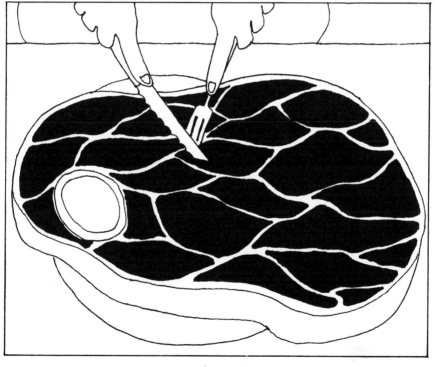

. . . it's protein

YOU'RE IN MOTION

YOU EAT IT
OFF THE FLOOR

. . . you're cooking

. . . your team is ahead

. . . your team is behind

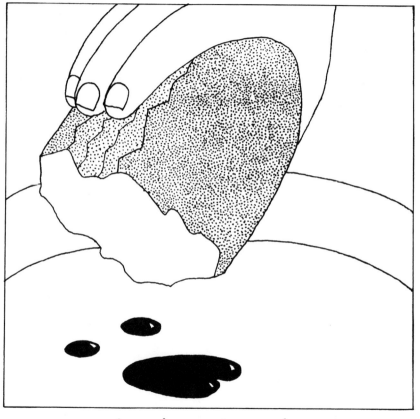

. . . you're only sopping up the gravy

THERE'S BEEN A NATURAL DISASTER

. . . you had no idea it had so many

. . . it's dry roasted

By now you have probably picked up the basic Positive Thinking Diet Plan, but you may have found a few situations a little hard to believe. This is understandable. Positive Thinking is very personal. What is truth for me is not necessarily truth for you. I'm sure that you've thought of a few times when "calories don't count" that I have neglected to put in this book. Good for you! You have gone a step beyond Positive Thinking and are on your way to a truly wonderful discovery — The Creative Thinking Weight Loss Plan.

The Creative Thinking Weight Loss Plan is based on the fact that you can *combine* your intuitive Calorie Facts to achieve a negative calorie count — no kidding. (On the opposite page there is a Calorie Fact Referral List. This is my personal list. You, of course, will make up one of your own.)

Let's start simply. Maybe you are not quite sure that one Calorie Fact is enough to secure a low calorie total, so, to cover yourself, you try eating frozen yogurt (1) for your late-night snack (2). Good! Or you make sure that your gift (3) is a box of dates (4). Very good.

Although there is no way to tell the precise moment when enough Calorie Facts combine to give you the minus calorie

Calories Don't Count When... (sara's list - Partial)

① It's anything made with yogurt.
② It's after 1:00 A.M.
③ It's a gift.
④ It's a fruit.
⑤ You're in motion.
⑥ You're on vacation.
⑦ You don't pay for it.
⑧ You're in a relative's home.
⑨ You have to demonstrate how good it is to the children.
⑩ It's protein.
⑪ Someone went to all that trouble.
⑫ It's shared.
⑬ You try something new.

⑭ You're in a foreign country.
⑮ Your team is winning.
⑯ The temperature is extreme.
⑰ You're standing up.
⑱ It tasted terrible.
⑲ It's health food.
⑳ You've just exercised.
㉑ You have a diet soda with your meal.
㉒ It's all you have.
㉓ You eat off someone else's plate.
㉔ It's a salad.
㉕ It's going to waste.

count (this is, after all, an inexact science), it is only logical that the more Calorie Facts you combine, the larger your minus calorie count will be.

Why not, if you are going on vacation (5), make it a fabulous ocean cruise (6)? See if you can get the captain to take you under his wing and pay for all your meals (7), many of which will be tropical fruit salads (4, 24).

Once you get the hang of this technique, it will almost become second nature to you. You could be at your aunt's (8) showing the children (9) how good the chopped liver (10) she went to all that trouble to make is (11), which is now going to waste (25). Maybe you share (12) a new taste treat (13) with a friend (7) in a foreign country (14). Of course, you are on vacation (5) while watching the national sport (15) in 101 degree weather (16). You both loved the game, stood up and cheered the whole time (17), but hated the whatever-it-was (18).

With this kind of imaginative thinking you can be thin as a rail inside a week!

You may ask at this point, "What about those situations when caloric intake is inevitable?" Did you forget that you promised to take Joe out to dinner for no special reason and you've already had two square meals?

Relax. It only appears hopeless. This is where you can really start to have fun with Creative Calorie Thinking. Maybe it's only a matter of choosing the correct place to eat. Take him to a health food restaurant (19).

"Yuck."

"Okay, Joe, a sushi bar." (10)

"Raw Fish?"

"All right, already, we'll try something new."

So you end up going to the Ivory Coast Barbeque. Just to be safe, you convince him to walk there (20).

"I think it's just a few more blocks."

If you are really wily, you might be able to trick him into take-out food that you'll eat while walking back (5).

"Gosh, Joe, it took so long to get here, it looks as though we'll have to head back right away."

But maybe you've unwittingly got yourself seated in a basic restaurant before you realize your predicament.

"Where am I?"

Hey, you're still okay. You may have to do a little fast talking.

"Would you like a little wine with your rack of lamb, sir?"

"No, I think I'll just have a Tab." (21)

"Hey, you know what would be fun? You order what I want and I'll order what you want. Then we'll eat off each other's plates! Ha ha ha ha ha!" (23)

"You're a real card."

"What a crazy time for my back to go out!"

"Do you want to go home?"

"No, I'll just have to eat standing up." (17)

But if worse comes to worst . . . "You're never going to believe this, Joe. It's so embarrassing! I've forgotten my wallet! Do you mind getting the check this time?" (7)

Now that's being resourceful. . . .

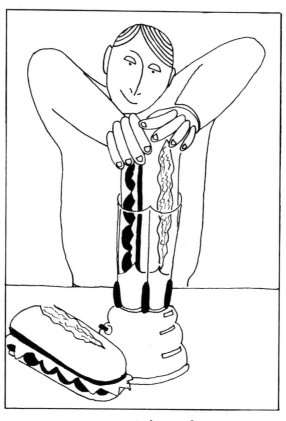

. . . it's liquid

YOU'RE
EATING
FOR
TWO

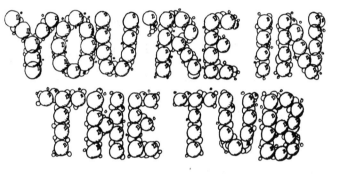

. . . the refrigerator door

is still open

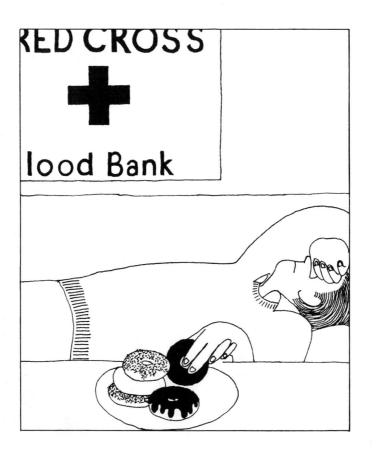

YOU'VE JUST

GIVEN BLOOD

. . . you don't know what else to do with your hands

. . . it's in lieu of worse things

SomeONE's
gone to all
That trouble.

you've already had **TOO MUCH**

. . . you're showing your kid how good it is

. . . you're starting your diet on Monday

IT'S YOUR BIRTHDAY